International Food Library

FOOD IN
KOREA

International Food Library

FOOD IN
KOREA

text by
Nancy Loewen

recipes compiled by
Judith A. Ahlstrom

Rourke Publications, Inc.
Vero Beach, Florida 32964

Library of Congress Cataloging-in-Publication Data

Loewen, Nancy, 1964-
    Food in Korea / by Nancy Loewen
       p.   cm. — (International food library)
    Includes index.
    Summary: Surveys food products, customs, and prepartion in Korea, describing typical dishes, cooking techniques, and recipes for a variety of meals.
    ISBN 0-86625-345-9
    1. Cookery, Korean—Juvenile literature.   2. Korea—Social life and customs—Juvenile literature.   3. Food habits—Korea—Juvenile literature.   [1. Cooking, Korean.   2. Food habits—Korea.
3. Korea—Social life and customs.]   I. Title.   II. Series.
TX724.5.K65L63   1991
641.59519—dc20   90-48798
                                                                          CIP
PRINTED IN THE USA   AC r912

CONTENTS

1. An Introduction to Korea   6

2. A Common Heritage   8

3. North and South Korea   10

4. Agriculture and Industry   12

5. Holidays in Korea   14

6. Food Customs in Korea   16

7. Korean Foods   18

8. A Festive Meal   20

9. A Red-Meat Meal   24

10. A White-Meat Meal   26

11. An Everyday Meal   28

     Glossary of Cooking Terms   29

     Korean Cooking   31

     Index   32

AN INTRODUCTION TO KOREA

In the mountains of South Korea, a family visits an ancient Buddhist temple. A statue of Buddha stands near a many-storied pagoda, its roof corners turning upward in graceful lines. The surrounding pine forests give the air a spicy, fresh scent.

The downtown streets of Seoul, South Korea, are filled with people and automobiles. A few people wear the colorful, flowing robes of the Korean tradition. Others wear blue jeans or business suits.

In rural North Korea, members of a farming cooperative wade through a rice paddy, harvesting the rice. In a nearby city, workers hurry to their jobs at a steel mill.

Korea is known for its serene landscape and traditions, as well as for its thriving industries. It is actually two countries, North Korea and South Korea. Together,

Songgwangsa Temple is one of South Korea's largest temple complexes. It is located in Mt. Chogyesan Park.

both countries make up the Korean Peninsula, a land mass that juts out of northeast China. The peninsula is about 670 miles long, and nearly 320 miles across at the widest point. The Sea of Japan lies to the east, and the Yellow Sea to the west. The Strait of Korea separates South Korea from the island nation of Japan.

North Korea is bordered on the north by China and the Soviet Union. It has a population of about 22,500,000. Pyongyang is the capital city. South Korea has a population of about 43,000,000. It includes nearly 3,000 small islands that lie off its western and southern shores. Seoul, the capital, was thrust into the world spotlight when South Korea hosted the 1988 Summer Olympic Games.

Much of Korea is mountainous, with fertile plains lining the coasts. The climate is affected by seasonal winds called monsoons. Summers in Korea are hot and humid, with a rainy season between June and August. Winters are generally cold and dry, although it does snow in the mountains.

A COMMON HERITAGE

The Korean Peninsula has a long and rich history. Choson, the first Korean state, was established in 2333 B.C. Throughout the centuries, Choson, and the Korean kingdoms that followed it, were invaded by the Chinese, Monguls, Manchus, and Japanese. The ideas and philosophies of these other nations—especially China—all contributed to today's Korean culture.

Religion, in particular, has had an important influence on the Korean people. The most ancient Korean religion is *shamanism*, or spirit worship. In shamanism, things such as rocks, mountains, and streams have spirits, just as people do. In times of trouble, a shaman priestess, called a *mudang*, tries to communicate with these spirits, or perhaps with the souls of ancestors. A shaman ceremony combines music, dance, and drama.

In the springtime, the grounds of Changdok-kung Palace in Seoul come alive with cherry and dogwood blossoms. The palace dates back to the 14th century and is the residence of the surviving royal family.

On Cheju Island, *tolharubang*—"rock grandfathers"—are a popular attraction. Long ago, the people of the islands looked to these unusual carved figures to protect them from harm.

Buddhism, an ancient religion that first emerged in India, was introduced to Korea in 372 A.D. by a Chinese Buddhist priest. For more than a thousand years, elements of Buddhism were present in Korean architecture and in the arts. Thousands of Buddhist temples were built, and many are still used today.

Another important influence was Confucianism, a social philosphy that was developed by Confucius, a scholar and statesman in ancient China. In 1392 A.D.—at the start of the Yi Dynasty—Confucianism became Korea's official religion. Confucian teaching emphasized ideas of duty and ethical behavior. The Korean tradition of honoring one's ancestors came from this philosophy.

In South Korea, many people still practice these traditional religions, as well as Christianity. In North Korea, the government discourages religious practices. About two-thirds of the North Korean people are atheists—that is, they don't believe in any sort of deity, or god. However, the influence of traditional religions is still apparent in Korean art, music, dance, and the attitudes and lifestyles of all the Korean people.

9

NORTH AND
SOUTH KOREA

For hundreds of years, the Koreans were united as one people. Events in the 20th century, however, have made major changes in Korea's political structure.

The Japanese took control of Korea in 1910, and remained in power for 35 years—until the end of World War II. Korea was liberated on August 15, 1945, when the Japanese surrendered to Allied forces. That didn't mean Korea was a free nation, however. After so many years of Japanese control, Korea's political system wasn't very strong. The northern half of Korea was soon occupied by communist forces from the Soviet Union, and the southern half by forces from the United States. Despite their common culture, the Korean people became alienated from each another.

The Freedom House in Panmunjom allows visitors a view of sealed-off North Korea.

South Korea—and its politics—received worldwide attention when Seoul hosted the 1988 Summer Olympics. Above is a formation of the official Seoul Olympic Emblem.

Two new governments—one for the North and one for the South—were set up in 1948, but each one claimed to govern the entire peninsula. In 1950, North Korea invaded South Korea, marking the start of the Korean War. The United Nations asked that member nations give aid to South Korea. The United States and other countries sent troops and supplies to South Korea, while North Korea was backed by China and the Soviet Union. The war—one of the bloodiest in recent times— ended in 1953 without a solution to the problem. U.S. troops are still stationed at the border between the two countries.

In North Korea, political elections are held, but all political power is centered in the Communist Party, called the Korean Workers' Party. In South Korea, there are many political parties. People elect the president as well as the members of the legislature, but there is still a great deal of political unrest.

Many Koreans support the idea of reunification. Discussions between the two nations have been held from time to time, but so far no real progress has been made.

AGRICULTURE & INDUSTRY

Throughout its history, Korea has been an agricultural society. Most Koreans lived in small villages and farmed the land with their families. This traditional lifestyle began to change in 1910, when Korea was under Japanese control. The changes became even more dramatic after World War II, when both countries made a determined effort to build up their industries. South Korea was influenced by the ideas and values of the United States and other Western nations. North Korea, on the other hand, was influenced by Communist thought.

Although the role of agriculture is changing in both countries, it is still very important. In North Korea, about 45 percent of the people work on government-run cooperative farms. Rice, corn, vegetables, potatoes, and fruits are the major crops. Most of the farming is done on the northwest plain.

Terraced rice paddies give a serene look to the Korean landscape.

Along the Korean coasts, fish are sold fresh off the docks.

In South Korea, agriculture employs 25 percent of the working population. Most farms are privately owned and quite small—averaging less than three acres in size. Crops include rice, barley, vegetables, and wheat. The best cropland is found along the western and southern coasts. On Cheju, Korea's largest island, oranges are grown.

Industry employs 25 percent of South Korean workers and 30 percent of North Korean workers. Both countries produce clothing and textiles, processed foods, and machinery. In South Korea, the manufacturing of electronic products (such as televisions and computers) has become a major industry in recent years.

Fishing, forestry, and mining are other important occupations on the rich Korean Peninsula. Oysters, pollack, and filefish are caught off the Korean coasts. Minerals include iron and copper ore, tungsten, limestone, and coal. In North Korea, hydroelectric power is another valuable resource. It is made possible by Korea's many rushing rivers.

HOLIDAYS IN KOREA

In Korea, holidays are a mix of time-honored traditions and modern celebrations. There are two calendars used in Korea: the Gregorian calendar (which is the one used in the United States and throughout most of the world), and an ancient Chinese calendar that is based on the cycles of the moon. Korea's older holidays are observed according to this lunar calendar.

The Korean New Year is officially celebrated on January 1. It is a time for families to get together. Younger people bow to their elders in a show of respect, and all family members honor their ancestors. The New Year may also be celebrated in January or February, according to the Chinese calendar. It is called Folklore Day.

A Korean family celebrates the New Year by playing a traditional game of *yut*. Players throw four wooden sticks into the air and are awarded points according to how the sticks land.

Festive lanterns abound on Buddha's birthday, observed in the spring.

Buddha's birthday is celebrated in the springtime, on the eighth day of the fourth lunar month. Koreans honor his birth by decorating Buddhist temples with candles or colorful paper lanterns, and by forming beautiful processions in the streets. This holiday is also called the Feast of Lanterns.

Chusok, the Korean Thanksgiving, is held in early fall, during the eighth lunar month. The celebration lasts for two days, during which time nearly all businesses shut down. During Chusok, Koreans may visit family tombs, bringing with them the foods and wines from harvest. Traditional costumes are worn, and there is much singing and dancing.

Two Korean holidays are especially fun for children. May 5 is Children's Day in Korea. This day is set aside to honor young people and to reaffirm the value of the family. Parents may take their children on family outings, and many children wear traditional costumes. *Tano*, or Swing Day, takes place in June. Dressed in their nicest clothes, many Korean girls take part in swinging contests.

15

FOOD CUSTOMS IN KOREA

Korean cuisine, both North and South, relies mainly on rice, meat, and vegetables. In many ways, it is similar to the cooking of China or Japan. Korean foods, however, tend to be spicier than other Oriental dishes. Red pepper is a popular seasoning. Soy sauce, garlic, sesame seeds, and ginseng are also commonly used. Many Koreans believe that ginseng can improve a person's health and slow down the aging process.

Because Koreans eat with chopsticks, meat and vegetables are usually cut into *julienne* strips—that is, cut into long, thin pieces. This makes the food easier to handle with chopsticks. It also allows food to cook more quickly, and emphasizes the various colors. A proper Korean meal will always include the colors red, green, white, yellow, and black. It will also have a variety of textures and flavors.

Variety—in color, flavor, and texture—is emphasized in a formal Korean meal, which can include up to 20 dishes.

These cooks are busy making *kimchi,* a staple food in Korea made from seasoned cabbage.

There are five main parts to a typical Korean meal: rice, soup, vegetables, the main course, and *kimchi.* The rice may be plain or perhaps mixed with beans, vegetables, or grains such as barley or wheat. The soup usually contains meat, seaweed, or fish. It may be thin, with clear broth as a base; or thick, with *tofu,* or bean paste, as a base. The main course features meat, poultry, or fish. Colorful side dishes called *panchan* are also present at Korean meals.

Kimchi is served at all Korean meals, including breakfast. The main ingredient in this traditional Korean dish is cabbage, which is fermented with red peppers, salt, and other seasonings. Kimchi may also contain vegetables such as turnips, cucumbers, or radishes, or perhaps bits of meat or fish. In the summer, kimchi is made every day. Winter kimchi, however, is usually made in autumn and is a project for the entire family. The kimchi is stored in large earthenware jars, and buried in the ground so that just the mouth of the jar is above the surface.

17

KOREAN FOODS

Korean food doesn't vary much from region to region, and the same foods may be served at breakfast, lunch, or dinner. However, there is still plenty of variety!

Beef dishes are very popular among Koreans. *Pulgogi*, or barbecued beef, is marinated in a sauce made of sesame oil, garlic, onion, sugar, pepper, and soy sauce. The meat is then broiled over a small charcoal grill, usually right at the table.

Pibim-bap is a hearty dish that combines rice, vegetables, meat, and beans. It is topped with a fried egg and often served with a spicy paste made of soybeans and red chile peppers. *Manduguk* is a soup made with meat-filled dumplings. *Samyetang* is a whole small chicken, stuffed with rice and ginseng and steamed in its own broth. These dishes are all likely to be found at Korean restaurants, as well as in Korean homes.

Korean shoppers are eager to buy rice, beans, and grains at an open market.

These workers are carefully harvesting tea leaves.

Panchan are the side dishes that are commonly served with Korean meals. There are all sorts of panchan. Many of these dishes are made with bean sprouts or seaweed, but other ingredients are common, too. *Shigumchi* is a leafy vegetable similar to spinach. It is blanched and seasoned with oil and sesame seeds. *Toraji*, Chinese bellflower root, and *kosari*, young fern fronds, are other popular vegetables.

In the summertime, *naengmyon* makes a refreshing meal. This is a cold soup made with buckwheat noodles and topped with bits of pear, cucumber, boiled eggs, and beef. The broth is seasoned with vinegar and mustard. A popular winter dish is *ttokkuk*, sliced rice cakes that have been boiled in beef broth. Ttokkuk is often served during New Year celebrations.

Koreans usually drink rice or barley tea with their meals, and dessert is likely to be fresh fruit. Treats such as cooked dried persimmons or date balls rolled in pine nuts may be served on special occasions.

A FESTIVE MEAL

Beef Soup
Bean Sprout Salad
Fried Shrimp
White Rice
Kimchi
Chestnut Balls

This fried shrimp takes some time to prepare, but it is probably some of the most tender and tasty shrimp you'll ever eat. All courses in this festive meal should be served together, except for the soup and dessert, which are served separately. The one item you have to make well ahead of time is the kimchi—it needs to marinate for several days.

Fried Shrimp

> *1 pound large raw shrimp*
> *salt and pepper to taste*
> *5 tablespoons flour*
> *2 eggs, beaten*
> *1/2 cup peanut oil*
> *4 tablespoons soy sauce*
> *1 tablespoon white vinegar*

1. Remove the shells from the shrimp. Using a small knife, remove the black vein if you like. Rinse the shrimp in cold water.
2. Slit the shrimp down the back—do not cut all the way through. Flatten them out on a cutting board. Sprinkle shrimp with salt and pepper, then coat them with flour.
3. Heat the oil in a skillet until hot. Dip each shrimp in the beaten eggs before placing in pan. Cook about 2 minutes on each side until golden brown. Drain on paper towels.
4. Mix the soy sauce and vinegar together in a small bowl. Serve this as a dipping sauce for the shrimp. Serves 4.

Fried Shrimp

Beef Soup

    1 1/2 pounds beef round steak, boneless
    6 cups cold water
    1 pound small turnips, peeled and sliced
    1 teaspoon black pepper
    1 tablespoon soy sauce
    1 teaspoon salt
    1 teaspoon finely chopped garlic
    1 tablespoon ground sesame seeds
    2 tablespoons chopped red bell pepper
    1 scallion, chopped

1. Trim fat off beef. Place in a large saucepan, cover with water, and set aside for 30 minutes.
2. Bring pan of meat and water to a boil. Add turnips and pepper. Cover and simmer for about 2 1/2 hours.
3. Remove meat from pot. Leave broth on low heat. Cut the beef into 3/4-inch cubes and put them into a soup tureen or serving bowl. Sprinkle with soy sauce, salt, garlic, sesame seeds, red pepper, and scallion. Mix well and let sit for 10 minutes.
4. Pour the hot broth and turnips over the meat and serve. Serves 4–6.

Bean Sprout Salad

  4 cups bean sprouts
  1 teaspoon soy sauce
  2 teaspoons white vinegar
  1 teaspoon sesame oil
  1/2 teaspoon sugar
  black pepper to taste
  2 green onions, thinly sliced
  2 radishes, grated
  2 teaspoons sesame seeds

1. Place bean sprouts in a large pan and cover with water. Bring to a boil, then immediately drain the sprouts using a colander or large strainer. Rinse with cold water and drain again.
2. Mix soy sauce, vinegar, oil, sugar, and pepper in a small bowl. Stir until sugar is dissolved.
3. Put sesame seeds in a dry frying pan. Toast them on medium heat, stirring constantly until the seeds are light brown and begin to "jump."
4. Mix sprouts, dressing, onions, radishes, and toasted sesame seeds in a large bowl. Serves 4.

White Rice

  2 cups rice
  2 cups water
  1/2 teaspoon salt
  1 teaspoon butter or oil

1. Place all ingredients in a heavy pan with a tight-fitting cover. Bring to a boil. Turn to low and simmer for 20 minutes or until water is absorbed. Serves 4.

Chestnut Balls

  2 cups chestnut puree
  pinch of ground ginger
  3/4 teaspoon ground cinnamon
  1/4 cup sugar
  1/2 cup honey
  1/2 cup almonds, finely chopped

1. Mix puree with ginger, cinnamon, and sugar.
2. Take a heaping teaspoon of the mixture and shape into balls. Dip into honey and roll in almonds.

Kimchi

> *2 pounds Chinese cabbage*
> *1/2 cup salt*
> *water*
> *2 tablespoons dried red pepper flakes*
> *1 clove garlic, chopped*
> *1 teaspoon fresh ginger, grated*
> *1 tablespoon sugar*
> *2 green onions, sliced thinly (including tops)*

1. Wash the cabbage in cold water. Cut into bite-size pieces. Put in large pan, sprinkle with salt, and cover with water. Set aside overnight.
2. Rinse the cabbage in cold water and drain.
3. In a glass or ceramic bowl, mix the cabbage with the other ingredients. Cover and place in refrigerator for 2–5 days. The longer the kimchi sits, the spicier it will be.

Kimchi

A RED-MEAT MEAL

Pulgogi
White Rice (see page 22)
Spinach Salad
Kimchi (see page 23)
Fresh Fruit

This meal features one of Korea's most famous dishes, pulgogi. In Korea, this spicy meat is cooked right on the table over a small barbecue grill. You can do the same, but it's easier to use your oven broiler. Serve everything together.

Pulgogi preparation: the unbeaten meat is on the left, and the beaten meat is on the right. In the bowl is the marinade.

Pulgogi

> 1 ¹/₂ *pounds beef tenderloin or sirloin steak*
> 2 *green onions, chopped*
> 2 *tablespoons finely chopped leek*
> 1 *shallot, finely chopped*
> 2 *cloves garlic, finely chopped*
> ¹/₂ *teaspoon sugar*
> 1 *teaspoon salt*
> ²/₃ *cup soy sauce*
> 2 *tablespoons sesame oil*
> 6–8 *drops Tabasco sauce*
> *Pulgogi sauce (see recipe next page)*

1. Cut the meat in thin slices, no more than ¼ inch thick. Then beat the slices with the bottom of a flat glass or jar until the meat is ⅛ inch thick. It helps to cover the meat with plastic wrap before beating.
2. Mix the green onions, leeks, shallot, garlic, sugar, salt, soy sauce, sesame oil, and Tabasco in a bowl. The more Tabasco you use, the hotter the beef will taste. Add the meat. Place in the refrigerator for 4 or more hours.
4. Preheat the broiler. Grill meat slices for 30 seconds on each side. Serve with pulgogi sauce. Serves 4.

Pulgogi Sauce

½ teaspoon salt
½ teaspoon sugar
1 teaspoon cayenne pepper
2 teaspoons sesame seeds
2 garlic cloves, minced
⅔ cup soy sauce
1 teaspoon minced onion
1 tablespoon sesame oil

1. Mix all ingredients in a small bowl. Serve at the table for dipping the meat.

Cooked Spinach Salad

¾ pound fresh spinach
1 teaspoon salt
6 cups water
3 tablespoons sesame seeds
3 tablespoons soy sauce

1. Wash the spinach. Cut or tear into small pieces. Boil in salted water for 3 minutes. Drain in colander or strainer. Put in refrigerator for 1 hour.
2. Put the sesame seeds in a dry frying pan. Toast them on medium heat, stirring constantly until the seeds are light brown and begin to "jump." Put seeds in a small bowl and crush with a heavy spoon. Add soy sauce and stir.
3. Toss spinach with dressing and serve. Serves 4.

A WHITE-MEAT MEAL

Stir-fried Chicken
Naengyon
White Rice (see page 22)
Kimchi (see page 23)
Fresh Fruit

Naengyon, a cold noodle soup, is another of Korea's well-known dishes. It's tasty and refreshing, especially on a hot day. All parts of this meal can be served together.

Stir-fried Chicken

    1 pound chicken breast, cut in 1-inch chunks
    1 teaspoon fresh ginger
    1 garlic clove, finely chopped
    4 tablespoons tomato paste
    1/2 teaspoon crushed red pepper
    2 tablespoons sesame oil
    2 carrots, sliced 1/8 inch thick
    1 green pepper, cut in 1-inch chunks
    1 medium onion, cut in 8 sections
    1 cup mushrooms, quartered
    1/4 cup water
    1 tablespoon corn starch

1. Combine chicken, tomato paste, oil, and spices in a bowl and let sit for half an hour.
2. Heat wok or large frying pan over high heat. Add chicken and cook 4 or 5 minutes.
3. Add vegetables and mushrooms and stir with the chicken. Cover and reduce heat to medium. Cook for about 30 minutes. Stir well, then cover and cook for 30 minutes more, or until carrots are done.
4. Mix cornstarch with 1/4 cup water in a cup. Pour it into the pan. Stir and simmer for 1 minute. Serve over rice. Serves 4.

Naengyon

Naengyon

> 1 8.8-ounce package thin buckwheat noodles
> 1 10 1/2 -ounce can beef broth
> 2 thinly sliced scallions or green onions
> 1/4 cup bean sprouts
> 1 sliced cucumber
> 1/4 pound cold beef slices (cooked)
> 3–4 radishes

1. Cook noodles according to directions. Drain in colander. Rinse with cold water for 2 minutes. Drain again.
2. Place noodles in large bowl. Pour beef broth over noodles. Top with onions, bean sprouts, cucumber, beef, and radishes. Chill for 1 hour. Serves 4.

AN EVERYDAY MEAL

Manduguk
White Rice (see page 22)
Kimchi (see page 23)

Making the wontons
for Manduguk is a
little tricky at first,
but it gets easier
after the first few
are made.

Manduguk

2 10 ½ -ounce cans beef broth
2 cans water
2 green onions or scallions, thinly sliced
1 carrot, grated
2 tablespoons sesame or peanut oil
⅓ cup chopped onion
⅓ pound ground beef
1 cup chopped cabbage
½ cup bean sprouts
a little black pepper, to taste
20–25 wonton skins
water for moistening skins

1. Bring first 4 ingredients to a boil in a large pot. Reduce heat and simmer 30 minutes.
2. Sauté the chopped onion in oil until clear and soft. Add the hamburger and cook until browned. Add the cabbage and cook, stirring frequently, about 3 minutes. Add the bean sprouts and cook 1–2 minutes more. Season with black pepper. Drain any fat.
3. Place wonton skin on a flat surface. Moisten edges with water, using your finger. Place 1 teaspoon filling in center of wonton skin. Lift four corners to the center and pinch edges together. Cover extra skins with a damp towel so they don't dry out.
4. Place wontons in hot broth, cover, and simmer for 20–30 minutes. *Do not boil!* Serves 4.

28

GLOSSARY OF COOKING TERMS

For those readers who are less experienced in the kitchen, the following list explains the cooking terms used in this book.

Chopped	Cut into small pieces measuring about ½ inch thick. Finely chopped pieces should be about ⅛ inch thick.
Diced	Cut into small cubes.
Garnished	Decorated.
Grated	Cut into small pieces by using a grater.
Greased	Having been lightly coated with oil, butter, or margarine to prevent sticking.
Knead	To work dough with one's hands.
Marinate	To cover and soak with a mixture of juices, called a marinade.
Minced	Chopped into very tiny pieces.
Pinch	The amount you can pick up between your thumb and forefinger.
Reserve	To set aside an ingredient for future use.
Sauté	To cook food in oil, butter, or margarine at high temperature, while stirring constantly.
Shredded	Cut into lengths of 1–2 inches, about ¼ inch across. Finely shredded ingredients should be about ⅛ inch across.
Simmer	To cook on a stove at the lowest setting.
Sliced	Cut into thin slices that show the original shape of the object.
Toss	To mix the ingredients in a salad.
Whisk	To beat using a hand whisk or electric mixer.

KOREAN COOKING

To make the recipes in this book, you will need the following equipment and ingredients, which may not be in your kitchen:

Almonds Can be found in the baking section of almost any grocery store.

Beef broth Can be found in the soup section of supermarkets.

Buckwheat noodles Most health-food stores and large supermarkets will have these noodles.

Chestnut puree Large supermarkets will have this item. You can make your own by putting fresh chestnuts (found in the produce section of large supermarkets) in a blender or food processor.

Garlic Fresh garlic can be bought in supermarkets. Each bulb can be broken into section called cloves. You have to remove the brittle skin around each cloved before chopping it. If you're feeling lazy, you can sometimes buy garlic that has already been chopped and put into small jars.

Produce Turnips, red bell peppers, scallions, bean sprouts, green onions, spinach, and shallots are found in the produce sections of most supermarkets.

Sesame oil This cooking oil can be found in most health-food stores and supermarkets. Korean grocery stores will always have it.

Spices Cinnamon, cayenne pepper, crushed red peppers, ground ginger, and marjoram wil be found in the spice section of supermarkets. Fresh ginger is found in the produce section of most supermarkets.

The choice of foods in Korea is simply amazing!

Wonton skins Most supermarkets will have this item in the produce section.

INDEX

Agriculture	12, 13	Recipes:	
		Bean Sprout Salad	22
Cheju	13	Beef Soup	21
Choson	8	Chestnut Balls	22
Climate	7	Cooked Spinach Salad	25
		Fried Shrimp	20
Diet	16, 17	Kimchi	23
		Manduguk	28
Festivals	14, 15	Naengyon	27
Fishing	13	Pulgogi	24
Fruit	12, 13, 19	Pulgogi Sauce	25
		Stir-fried Chicken	26
Government	11	White Rice	22
		Religion	8, 9
Herbs	16, 31		
		Samyetang	18
Industry	12, 13	Sea of Japan	7
		Seoul	6
Manduguk	18	South Korea	6, 7, 9, 10, 11, 13
Minerals	13	Spices	16, 17, 19, 31
		Strait of Korea	7
North Korea	6, 7, 9, 10, 11, 12		
		Ttokkuk	19
Panchan	19		
Pibim-bap	18	Vegetables	12, 13, 17, 19
Population	7		
Pulgogi	18	Yellow Sea	7
Pyongyang	7		

We would like to thank and acknowledge the following people for the use of their photographs and transparencies:

Mark E. Ahlstrom: cover inset, 21, 23, 24, 27, 28; Korea National Tourism Corporation: cover, 2, 7, 8, 9, 10, 11, 12, 13, 14, 15, 16, 17, 18, 19, 30.

Produced by Mark E. Ahlstrom (The Bookworks)
Typesetting and layout by The Final Word
Photo research by Judith Ahlstrom